Test Lean and Ship Healthy: A Handbook on Delivering High Quality Software in the DevOps World

Asankhaya Sharma   Darius Foo   Hendy Chua

Jason Yeo   Andrew Santosa   Jonah Dela Cruz

ii

Contents

Introduction

Shipping code fast is key to delivering a successful software product. First-mover advantage is critical in many domains, and with the easy availability of cloud infrastructure, open source components, and CI/CD practices and tools, it's never been more possible to go fast.

However, increasing speed at the cost of everything else ("move fast and break things") is untenable beyond a certain point. When shortcuts are taken, tech debt accumulates, slowing development over time. Furthermore, the occasional bug or incident must be tolerable – a non-starter in domains where availability is paramount, e.g. cloud infrastructure, or application security products.

This seems at first glance like a fundamental tradeoff, but doesn't have to be: if processes and tools evolve to support rapid development, we *can* maintain quality while shipping on time. The key is being extremely deliberate with our testing efforts and continuously optimizing them for efficiency.

Effective and Efficient Testing

Traditional software development models rely heavily on black box integration (or *system*) testing: running test cases against live instances of the application with real databases attached, usually in some sort of staging environment.

Indicators that this is the case include having dedicated "QA engineers" who spend most of their time writing tests, the use of a test case management system, or there being a special testing phase, usually occurring after development on a feature is done and before release.

This isn't a bad thing in itself, but it does reveal that testing is seen as something separate from the development process. Is *this* a bad thing?

The following histogram, taken from a study[^1] on software quality metrics, shows the distribution of bugs across 114 projects and the phase of development in which they were identified.

Of note is the low *effectiveness* of system testing; most bugs were detected via other means, *throughout development*.

Later in the paper, we see a plot of bugfix time by development phase.

It is also significantly less *efficient* to fix a bug past the development phase due to the overhead involved. Testing late is prohibitively expensive:

> The difficulty is that a system must be tested, unexpected results logged in the bug-tracking system, the issue must be assigned, the actual source of the fault must be identified before the problem can be corrected, and finally the fix must be retested. High [bugfix] yields are only possible when there are very few defects entering late test since high defect rates would overwhelm the capacity to execute the find, fix it, and retest.

Whereas if a bug were found via a unit test, a developer could fix it in minutes and move on.

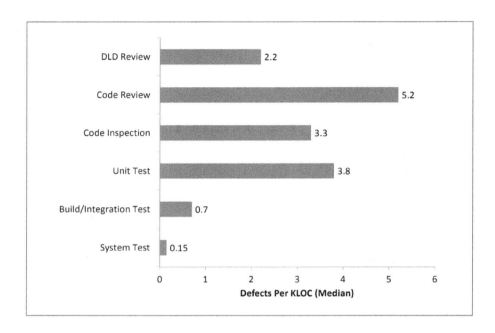

Figure 1: ineffectiveness of testing

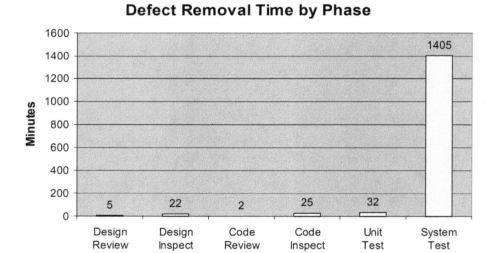

Figure 2: inefficiency of testing

A conclusion we can draw from this is that testing *has* to be interleaved with development if we are to get a significant quality yield from it. Quality cannot be "tested in" at the end; it is an integral part and consequence of the development process.

This is not to say that integration testing should not be used. It can be useful as a sanity check (in the form of smoke tests), but there is little reason to use it as the primary form of testing. Unit testing is vastly more effective at finding some kinds of bugs (e.g. errors in method-level specifications), and being significantly cheaper than integration testing, it should be used whenever it suffices; at the same time, it should not be used to the exclusion of other techniques (e.g. exclusively doing TDD). This argument can be made for most of the multitude of testing techniques in use today. In fact, the more diverse our testing strategy, the more mileage we're likely to get out of it.

In this book, we cover a number of these techniques, including:

- **Extensions to unit testing**: property-based testing and test case generation
- **Lightweight integration testing**: functional testing/BDD, contract testing, regression testing
- **Integration testing**: tools for writing them more correctly and efficiently
- **Exhaustive testing**: fuzzing, proving correctness

Quality as Availability

Users experience the robustness of a system through its availability, which is typically characterized by two metrics:

- The *mean time between failures* (MTBF) is the average amount of a time the system is able to function correctly for. It measures how reliable the system is.
- The *mean time to repair* (MTTR) measures the average amount of downtime. It also serves as a proxy for how reactive the team is to failures and how efficiently they are resolved.

Availability (or uptime) is thus

$$Availability = \frac{MTBF}{MTBF + MTTR}$$

For example, if a system fails every 10 hours for 15 minutes each time on average, its availability would be $\frac{10}{10+0.25} = 97.6\%$.

How does this relate to testing? *Testing is only ever able to increase MTBF.* No amount of testing can *prevent* a system from going down or shorten the amount of time it spends broken. We're reminded of Dijkstra's well-known quote:

> Program testing can be used to show the presence of bugs, but never to show their absence!

This means that beyond a certain point, testing will not increase availability.

For the given MTTR values, as MTBF increases, even to the extent of years, the graphs all converge and availability stops increasing. If we want to achieve high availability, we need *monitoring* in addition to testing, to reduce MTTR – ways to find or react to bugs, not just check for them.

A corollary to this is that exhaustive testing or optimizing for coverage isn't the most cost efficient use of time for availability. Given that there is very limited time for software quality in general, we have to be very careful how we spend it.

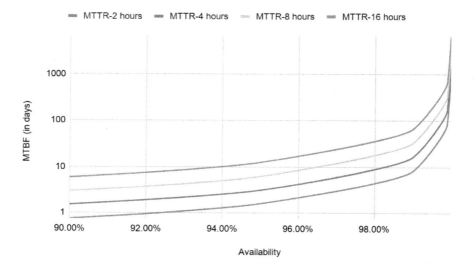

Figure 3: achieving high availability

Testing + Monitoring

The approach to testing we outlined is often referred to as "Shifting Left", in reference to the waterfall diagram we know and love.

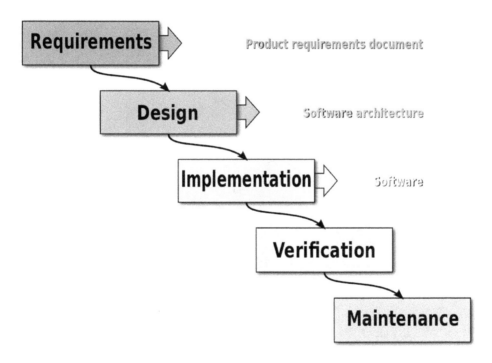

Figure 4: waterfall

The idea is to move testing to the left, to an earlier stage in the development process.

In striving to reduce MTTR and pursue greater levels of availability, we might suggest Shifting Right as well, past the deployment phase, when we implement a monitoring strategy. This would include:

- **Ways to deploy more robustly**: atomic deployments, automated rollbacks
- **Ways to find bugs**: chaos engineering
- **Ways to contain blast radius**: feature flags, dark releases, canary deployments, circuit breaking
- **Ways to be alerted faster**: metrics, alarms

Implementing these competently makes it possible for us to have both high quality and speed.

Principles

In conclusion, here are the principles of our approach.

Complete automation over manual testing

- Deployments and infrastructure should be fully automated and transparent
- Any engineer on the team should be able to deploy
- Automated quality gates (static analysis, security scans, passing tests) should be kept relevant
- Break builds to uphold standards
- Constant reevaluation of pipeline speed and quality gate relevance
- No manual testing
- No manual gatekeeping (except for code review)

Early error detection over end-to-end testing

- Quality cannot be "tested in"
- Testing must be interleaved with development
- An ensemble of testing techniques is more effective and efficient
- All developers are involved in writing and maintaining tests

Monitoring and recovery over exhaustive testing

- Testing only increases MTBF, which cannot increase availability beyond a certain point
- Reducing MTTR via monitoring is required for high availability
- Exhaustive testing isn't a cost efficient way to increase quality

Increasing confidence in delivery over bug finding

To quote John Regehr:

The market for software, generally speaking, does not reward correct software so much as software that is acceptably correct and that can be built cheaply and rapidly. Thus, while our work on software correctness is highly unlikely to improve the quality of software, it may plausibly make it possible to create acceptable software a bit more cheaply and rapidly.

No amount of testing can show that a system is free of bugs. However, the purpose of testing in a commercial software environment is not to produce flawless software, but to increase confidence in delivery: to give us assurance that our software can not only evolve correctly, but work correctly in the hands of real users.

To that end, we employ the same methods and tools and strive towards the same ideals, but are willing to compromise rigor when that would impede delivery.

Beyond Unit Tests: Automated Test Case Generation

Unit testing is an important aspect of software development. Having a proper test suite for your project can help detect bugs early and prevent regressions. Wouldn't it be great if we could generate unit test cases automatically? Well, it is certainly possible and I will explain in this article how you can do so for Java.

Recently, I had a chance to look at unit test case generation for Java. I had forked an old cross platform serialization library wox and it did not come with a test suite. I had to make a few changes and fix some bugs in the library to make it work with the current version of Java platform. I wanted to ensure that the changes I made did not break any existing functionality. Since the wox library did not come with its own set of test cases it was difficult to check that no regression bugs were introduced.

After searching online, I found an automated test suite generation framework for Java - EvoSuite. The EvoSuite framework automatically generates test cases for Java classes based on maximizing a coverage criteria, like branch coverage. I used their standalone jar to add a test suite to the wox library. It was surprisingly easy to set up and use.

In order to generate the test suite we use the following command:

```
java -jar evosuite.jar -generateTests <target> [options]
```

The <target> can be either a jar file of a folder containing your class files. This would generate the test cases in a folder named "evosuite-tests" in the current directory. The test cases generated use JUnit and can be run separately from an IDE as well. The [options] control various parameters including coverage criteria, the default criteria is branch coverage. Thus the generated tests cover all the branches in the methods. If you are using some external library then make sure that it is available in the class path otherwise EvoSuite will not be able to create test cases with objects that are defined in that library. This is

13

because to create objects during generation of test cases EvoSuite needs to call appropriate constructors for those objects.

For test case generation, EvoSuite has a bunch of different strategies including *search-based* and *constraint-based* algorithms.

- *Search Based Test Generation* : Uses a genetic algorithm to evolve the population of candidate test cases that satisfy a particular fitness function

- *Constraint Based Test Generation* : Uses symbolic execution to generate constraints and solve those constraints to explore different paths in the program.

Their ASE 2011 paper explains both the above techniques and how they can be combined and used together.

In terms of the quality of the automated generated test cases, it seems to do a good job of capturing the current behavior of the methods while providing good branch coverage. As an example consider the following method from the **wox.serial.Util** class :

```java
/**
 * Returns true if the class which name is passed as parameter is <i>stringable</i>.
 * In other words, returns true if objects of the class can go easily to a string
 * representation.
 * @param name The name of the class to test.
 * @return True if the class is stringable. False otherwise.
 */
public static boolean stringable(String name) {
    try {
        Class realDataType = (Class)TypeMapping.mapWOXToJava.get(name);
        //if the data type was found in the mapWOXToJava then it is "stringable"
        if (realDataType!=null){
            return true;
        }
        else{
            return false;
        }
    } catch(Exception e) {
        return false;
    }
}
```

The **stringable** method has two branches that correspond to whether the input **name** can be converted to a string by the **mapWOXToJava.get** method. EvoSuite generates the following two test cases for this method. **test02** covers the branch where the conditional is true whole **test03** covers the else branch. Also note that it is automatically able to create the inputs for **name** argument that drive the execution to the different branches.

```java
//Test case number: 2
/*
 * 1 covered goal:
 * 1 wox.serial.Util.stringable(Ljava/lang/String;)Z: I10 Branch 21 IFNULL L125 - false
 */

@Test
public void test02()  throws Throwable  {
    boolean boolean0 = Util.stringable("charWrapper");
    assertEquals(true, boolean0);
```

```
}

//Test case number: 3
/*
 * 1 covered goal:
 * 1 wox.serial.Util.stringable(Ljava/lang/String;)Z: I10 Branch 21 IFNULL L125 - true
 */

@Test
public void test03()  throws Throwable  {
    boolean boolean0 = Util.stringable("2p8f2V@rzS");
    assertEquals(false, boolean0);
}
```

You can have a look at the entire test suite generated for the wox library at the
GitHub repo. For the purpose of creating a regression test suite for a library
that did not have one it seems to be quite effective. Now, if I make some changes
in the wox library I can run the tests again and check if leads to any test failures.
In general, automated test cases may not be as good as hand written ones.
Another potential issue is the evolution of the test suite. Generating new tests
with EvoSuite for each release may not be the right thing to do. Nevertheless
the automated test suite can be used as a base for writing your own more
comprehensive test cases, which is what I plan to do with the wox library.

There are several other tools (under active development) for Java that also
produce automated unit test cases. I haven't had a chance to use them yet but
I list them here for reference - CATG, Randoop and Symbolic Pathfinder. An
experience report, titled EvoSuite at the Second Unit Testing Tool Competition
provides more details on using EvoSuite and how it compares with other similar
tools.

Beyond Unit Tests: Property-based Testing

Expressing Program Behaviours

In a previous article, we looked at the use of EvoSuite framework for automated test case generation in Java. As mentioned in that article, EvoSuite uses *search-based* and *constraint-based* methods for generation of test cases. These methods are guided by coverage criteria (e.g. branch coverage) and ability to explore different paths in the program. The test cases generated by these methods may not capture the intended behavior of the program. In today's article we will see how we can generate test cases that capture certain behaviors about programs. This can be done using *property-based* testing.

JUnit-QuickCheck is a library that provides *property-based* testing for Java programs. It is inspired by the QuickCheck library for Haskell that first pioneered this approach for automated testing. The library makes use of JUnit's Theory feature to support parameterized test cases. These test cases allow the developer to specify the property that the method under test should satisfy. JUnit-QuickCheck then uses randomly generated values to test the property. The following example shows how to use the @Theory annotation to specify a test method:

```
@RunWith(Theories.class)
public class PropertyJUnitTest {
  @Theory public void testEncodeBase64(@ForAll byte [] src){
    byte [] ec = EncodeBase64.encode(src);
    byte [] dec = EncodeBase64.decode(ec);
    Assert.assertArrayEquals(src,dec);
  }
}
```

This unit test is calling the `encode` and `decode` functions of the `EncodeBase64` class from the wox cross platform serialization library. The property of interest here is that `encode` is *invertible*, with `decode` as its inverse, i.e. x = decode(encode(x)). In other words, we want to check that encoding a byte array and then decoding it back leads to the same byte array. The `assertArrayEquals` at the last line ensures that this property is satisfied. This property is tested by

17

randomly generating a large number (100 by default) of byte arrays and calling
the `testEncodeBase64` with those values as input. The `@ForAll` annotation
is provided by the JUnit-QuickCheck library and takes care of generating the
appropriate random inputs.

If there are two inputs to the method, then all possible combinations of the
randomly generated inputs are tested. In order to avoid running so many tests
we can specify constraints on the input as shown below:

```
@Theory
public void testEncodeBase64withLength(@ForAll byte [] src) {
  assumeThat(src.length, greaterThan(32));
  byte[] ec = EncodeBase64.encode(src);
  byte[] dec = EncodeBase64.decode(ec);
  Assert.assertArrayEquals(src,dec);
}
```

The `assumeThat` ensures that only byte arrays with length greater than 32 are
generated. The library already comes with generators for all primitive Java
types and there is also a separate module `junit-quickcheck-guava` containing
generators for Guava types. However, if we need to generate inputs of custom
type we need to provide a generator. It can be done by extending the `Generator`
class and overriding the `generate` method. The following example shows one
possible way to generate random inputs of the `org.jdom2.Element` type.

```
public class ElementGenerator extends Generator<Element> {

  public ElementGenerator() {
    super(Element.class);
  }

  @Override
  public Element generate(SourceOfRandomness rand, GenerationStatus gs) {
    Element e = new Element(RandomStringUtils.randomAlphabetic(16));
    int numofAttr = rand.nextInt(8);
    for(int i=0; i<numofAttr; i++) {
      e.setAttribute(RandomStringUtils.randomAlphabetic(8),RandomStringUtils.randomAlphabetic(8));
    }
    e.addContent(RandomStringUtils.randomAlphabetic(rand.nextInt(16)));
    return e;
  }
}
```

Every time the `generate` method is called, it creates a random alphabetic string
that is used as the name of the element and adds up to 8 random attribute
values in it. To use this generator for the `Element` type we need to specify the
class with the `@From` annotation after the `@Forall` in the test method as shown
below:

```
@Theory
public void testElement2String(
  @ForAll @From(ElementGenerator.class) Element e)
  throws Exception {
  String s = element2String(e);
  // ...
}
```

The use of custom generators allows us to use *property-based* testing for arbitrary
classes and methods with little effort. The source code for all the tests is available

under the wox repository on GitHub. In addition, some other frameworks (under active development) providing similar functionality for Java are Quickcheck and ScalaCheck. However, JUnit-QuickCheck is the only one to use the Theory support in JUnit which makes it a lot easier to integrate in the development workflow.

Checking Informal Specifications

Property-based testing shifts our focus from simple assertions about values to logical *properties* that code should satisfy. Another use is checking informal, natural-language specifications; translating these statements into logical terms allows us to leverage a property-based test to check them.

One of the building blocks we implemented building SourceClear was a library for interpreting CVSS, a set of metrics used to assess the severity of software vulnerabilities.

The textual encoding of a set of CVSS metrics is called a *vector*:

`AV:A/AC:L/Au:N/C:P/I:P/A:C/E:ND/RL:OF/RC:ND/CDP:H/TD:M/CR:ND/IR:ND/AR:H`

Vectors are structured, consisting of several *metric groups*.

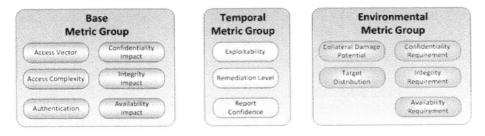

Figure 5: CVSS metric groups

Furthermore, there are many rules governing the relationships between metric groups and values, specified informally. Both of these make it a prime candidate for property-based testing.

We start by defining data structures and generators for vectors:

```
class CVSSVector {
  BaseVector baseVector;
  TemporalVector temporalVector;
  EnvironmentalVector environmentalVector;
}

public class CVSSVectorGenerator extends Generator<CVSSVector> {
  @Override
  public CVSSVector generate(SourceOfRandomness rand, GenerationStatus gs) {
    return gen().fieldsOf(CVSSVector.class).generate(rand, gs);
  }
}
```

As this library parses and pretty-prints vectors, we test a simple property of the *implementation*: that parsing is invertible, with pretty-printing as its inverse:

```
@Property
public void cvssVectorInvertible(CVSSVector cvssVector) throws ParseException {
  assertEquals(cvssVector, new CVSSVector(cvssVector.toString()));
}
```

So far so good.

CVSS also defines a means of turning a vector into a numeric score, allowing vectors to be ordered (and vulnerabilities prioritized). We transcribe the equations faithfully, then test a simple property from the spec relating the scores of the base and temporal metric groups:

```
/**
 * ... the temporal equation will combine the temporal metrics with the base score
 * to produce a temporal score ranging from 0 to 10. Further, the temporal score will
 * produce a temporal score no higher than the base score, and no greater than 33% lower
 * than the base score.
 */
@Property
public void temporalScoreRange(BaseVector baseVector, TemporalVector temporalVector) throws ParseException {
    double temporal = temporalVector.getScore(baseVector);
    assertTrue(0 <= temporal && temporal <= 10);
    assertTrue(temporal <= baseVector.getScore());
    double baseThreshold = baseVector.getScore() * (1 - 0.33);
    assertTrue(temporal <= baseThreshold);
}
```

Surprisingly, the third assertion fails and a counter-example is printed:

```
java.lang.AssertionError: Property temporalScoreRange falsified.
Args: [AV:A/AC:L/Au:N/C:P/I:P/A:N, E:H/RL:OF/RC:UR]
```

Our first thought is that the implementation is wrong in some way. Perhaps floating-point error? We check two other implementations of CVSS2 scoring and see the same result: a base score of 4.8, a temporal score of 4.0, and the impossible assertion `4.0 < 4.8 * (1-0.33)`.

Looking at the temporal equation analytically, we see that the minimum temporal score is:

```
temporal = base * min(exploitability) * min(remediationLevel) * min(reportConfidence)
         = base * 0.85 * 0.87 * 0.9
         = base * 0.67 (2 d.p.)
```

In other words, "33% lower than the base score" is the *lower bound*. Clearly the spec should have said **no smaller than**, i.e. `base * (1-0.33) <= temporal <= base`. Note also the inconsistent uses of *higher* and *greater*, and the difficulty of parsing that sentence in general; issues like these illustrate why natural language should be kept to a minimum in specifications.

We continue transcribing and testing, and find a similar error in the computation for the environmental score.

```
/**
 * ... the environmental equation will combine the environmental metrics with the temporal
 * score to produce an environmental score ranging from 0 to 10. Further, this equation will
 * produce a score no higher than the temporal score.
 */
```

```
@Property
public void environmentalScoreRange(BaseVector baseVector, TemporalVector temporalVector,
                         EnvironmentalVector environmentalVector) throws ParseException {
    double environmentalScore = environmentalVector.getScore(baseVector, temporalVector);
    assertTrue(0 <= environmentalScore && environmentalScore <= 10);
    assertTrue(environmentalScore < temporalVector.getScore(baseVector));
}

java.lang.AssertionError: Property environmentalScoreRange falsified.
Args: [AV:N/AC:M/Au:M/C:P/I:C/A:P, E:H/RL:ND/RC:UR, CDP:LM/TD:ND/CR:M/IR:M/AR:M]
```

Here the equations are given in terms of both the base and temporal scores, and consequently the cause of the error is much less obvious, demonstrating the value of the property-based approach.

The interesting thing about this example is that it shows that once the implementation is correct (e.g. comparable to another implementation), the property-based test extends to a test of the *specification*.

This idea is very similar to grammar-based fuzzing, which we'll cover next.

Execute Your User Stories!

Let's build something!

```
Product Owner: "Let's build something that brings me across the Atlantic Ocean."
Developer: (Builds a plane...)
Product Owner: "Uh... I actually just needed a ship."
Developer: Uh... ok...
```

Although the above scenario sounds contrived, this happens a lot on a smaller scale in software teams. Requirements from product management are sometimes poorly specified, causing developers to have to guess what's on the product owner's mind. This leads to developers coming up with products that are over-engineered or worse; the implementation sometimes misses the mark and fails to build the intended product.

What can we do about it?

We need something to bridge the gap between the product owner and the developer. Something that can describe exactly what is being built so everyone is on the same page and no effort is wasted. A tool that tries to solve this is Cucumber. Cucumber is a testing tool that supports behavior driven development (BDD), an extension of test driven development (TDD). In TDD, developers write tests before writing code, whereas in BDD, the specifications (or behaviors, hence BDD) are written before code is written. These specifications are what the user actually wants in the product. In Cucumber, these feature specifications are usually written by the product owner in collaboration with the development team. The developers would then implement them. The specifications can then be executed with Cucumber to ensure that they are working as intended. In some sense, the specifications are now the tests and they can be run as part of the CI pipeline.

In summary a BDD cycle would look like this:

- Product owner writes feature specifications in collaboration with the development team.

- Developers implement the feature.
- Cucumber tests are executed in CI to ensure specifications were met.

Example of a feature specification

In Cucumber, product specifications are written in features files using a Domain-specific Language (DSL) known as Gherkin. In its simplest form, Gherkin programs consist of a series of Given-When-Then clauses that are close to natural language. Here's an example of a feature file in Cucumber that specifies a feature for a calculator program:

```
Feature: Addition
  Scenario: Calculate the sum of two integers
    Given two integers
    When the add button is pressed
    Then the sum of the two integers should be displayed
```

Being very close to natural language, it is readable by stakeholders in the organization and non-technical product owners. In the above example it is clear how the user is interacting with the program, what the inputs and preconditions are, and what should be expected. These properties are described using the Given-When-Then language:

- `Given`: describes the preconditions of the feature
- `When`: describes the action that the user carries out in the feature
- `Then`: desribes what's expected after the action is performed

In Cucumber, these are known as steps. Each step when evaluated has a predefined behavior. Although Cucumber comes with some predefined steps, developers can extend the language to suit their applications. For example, the following step uses the `click_on` method defined in the `capybara` ruby gem. It navigates to the home page when Cucumber sees a step that says `When the home button is clicked`:

```
When(/^the home button is clicked$/) do
  click_on 'Home'
end
```

Executable user stories

In an agile team, this feature file is also known as a user story. It defines a user's requirements in the way the user would interact with the software. Apart from being a document to communicate the requirements of a user, this feature file can be executed and run against the product to ensure that the product meets the user's requirements and use cases as described in the story. To do so, Cucumber evaluates the Gherkin language, populates the test environment with the preconditions and input, simulates the interaction with the program, and lastly checks the actual behavior of the program against the desired behavior as specified in the feature file.

Closing thoughts

Cucumber and BDD close the gap between the non-technical requirements and technical implementation. They also close the gap between the product owners and the developers. When writing in Gherkin, software teams have to think about the requirements in a user-centric way. Requirements are no longer just "Build a calculator that adds"; with Given-When-Then clauses, developers have to think harder about preconditions, inputs, and expectations of each feature. What's more, with Cucumber, these files are executable, thus ensuring that the working implementation of the program runs exactly in the way that is described in the feature file.

Where is My Cassette?
Mocking System Testing

Introduction

Software Composition Analysis (*SCA*) has gained traction in industry with offerings from various companies. It helps developers identify vulnerable open-source libraries used in the software they develop. The following picture shows the architecture of an SCA system:

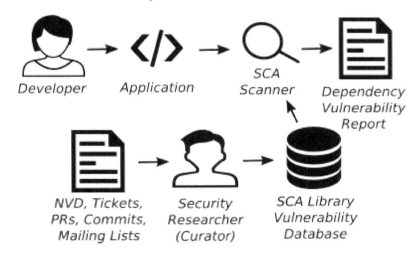

Figure 6: Software Composition Analysis System

In an SCA system, a customer scans their applications using a scanner software, which will then send the evidence of third-party dependencies to a server for matching with known vulnerabilities, whose data stored in a vulnerability database. The vulnerability database itself is curated by a team security researchers in years.

Veracode provides an *Agent-Based Scan* service using a *Command-Line Interface*

(*CLI*) agent that the customers run on their own machines to scan for vulnerable libraries used by their applications. The SCA CLI agent sends the evidence of third-party libraries to a data server, which matches them with known vulnerable libraries in the database.

Veracode's CLI agent runs on the customer's side, and it is important to ensure that it works correctly, given the environment the customer runs the agent in. There are three kinds of automated testing that we perform for the CLI agent:

1. *Unit testing*, which is the test that the output or behavior of methods are correct, given some input.

2. *Integration testing*, which is to actually execute the agent in various configurations, but scanning mocks instead of actual projects. Here we observe the actual output of the agent, such as its return value. There is no actual communication with the SCA vulnerability database server.

3. *System testing*, which is to actually execute the agent for scanning real projects and observe its behavior. Here the test checks the correctness of the actual messages sent by the agent to the server, which constitute the output of the agent.

In this article we discuss our approach to system testing, which, in order to test for the output correctness, generates checks using a *capture* mechanism and perform the actual test using a *replay* mechanism. The advantage of using such mechanisms is that it allows us to *mock* the SCA server and the library repositories during agent run, such as when issues are detected by the tests, we will be able to immediately localize as an issue belonging to the agent itself. As at the time of writing, for Veracode agent-based scan, the system testing has been implemented for real project scans on the Linux platform, and the same for Windows platform is planned.

Testing Objectives

Testing can be done for various purposes, such as for testing the usability and performance of the software being developed. Here our strategic purpose of performing system testing is to detect *regression*, that is, the reduction in the quality of the CLI agent, which potentially happens as the agent is being updated. Particularly, with our system testing we want to ensure that the CLI agent and the SCA server, as well as the library repositories work well together, particularly after making updates to the source code of the CLI agent.

The technical objectives include two:

- To ensure that the agent actually performs the computation that we expect of it. That is, for *validation*.

- To ensure that the result of the computation is what we expect. That is, for *ensuring correctness*.

It should be obvious that the major limitation of testing is in the limited number of ways we can validate or ensure correct the software under test. We cannot ensure that the software will be have correctly if the particular behavior is untested. In other words, it is unable to ensure that something unexpected will never happen.

Testing is typically done by executing the software or part of it, and observe the outcome. Validation can be performed by observing that the execution does reach some favorable end points (no exceptions, hangs, etc., unless these are what we test the software for), whereas correctness can be determined by observing that whenever a favorable end state is reached, the computation result matches expectation.

Capture and Replay

The following message sequence chart shows a simplification of the interactions among the CLI agent, the SCA server, and the library repository (e.g., Maven central, PyPi, etc.) when the CLI agent scans a repository:

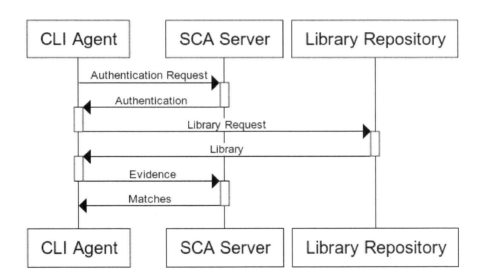

Figure 7: CLI Agent Interaction with the SCA Server

The purpose of our system testing is to test the interactions between the SCA system's components, where it needs to check that the proper interaction is actually performed (validation), and that the content of the interaction is as expected (correctness). The CLI agent is a highly complex software, which limits us into performing black-box testing only. In black-box testing, we check for the outputs of the system under test without considering the implementation details of the system itself. Therefore, when scanning a project implemented in a particular language or build system, we test that *the CLI agent sends the correct requests* to the SCA server. This is because we consider the requests to be the outputs of the CLI agent. As we can see here, we perform validation by observing that the CLI agent actually sends the requests during its execution, and we ensure correctness by observing that each time the CLI agent sends a request, it sends the *correct* one.

Here we need to define what is a correct request. We define a *correct* request to be a request that matches our record, when the same project was scanned last. Therefore, there is a need to store the requests for a successful run once, for comparison with subsequent runs.

Not only the requests, we also need to record the responses sent back by the SCA server and the library repository to the CLI agent. These responses are from the previous successful run, so that when the failure occurs in repeat runs, we can isolate the cause to be that of the CLI agent and not due to changes and failures in the remote systems (the SCA server or the library repository).

The system testing framework thus supports two separate activities:

1. The *capture* of the interactions (requests and responses). Here, `mitmdump` from the mitmproxy suite is used. `mitmdump` is started with a custom script that logs all requests and responses to JSON files. In this activity, the framework executes the agent and records the agent's HTTP requests, together with the QA SCA server's and library repository's responses. The raw requests and responses are collated into a *cassette* (so they can later be replayed without actually contacting the servers) and a JSON file containing all requests made.

2. The *replay* of the interactions (requests and responses) for testing. This is the actual test execution. Here, when the agent sends a request, the request reaches a local proxy (`mitmdump`), which then forwards it to a local mock server, implemented using Sinatra. The local server then responds to the CLI agent by sending the recorded responses in the cassette back to it, via the proxy. When the CLI sends an evidence query to the server, the framework tests that the query matches the recorded, previously-sent query during the capturing process.

An important thing to remember here is that the agent does not test for the consistency of the responses from the SCA server and the library repository with previously-recorded responses. That is, the previously-recorded responses are only used for replaying the responses of the SCA server and the library repository to the CLI agent. This is because **the test subject is the CLI agent**, and therefore we focus our effort in matching the requests with the recorded requests, since the requests are the outputs of the agent.

The CLI agent supports scanning projects implemented using a variety of languages and build systems from Java Maven projects to Objective-C with Co-

coapods and even C/C++ with `make`. Due to a large number and variety of tests, the scanned projects are divided into test *suites* for which currently there are 17. The suites and the functional testing are executed in parallel (whenever CPU resources are available) in the Gitlab CI. The name of the CI test job indicates the kind of repositories that are scanned by the CLI agent for testing. The following shows all the suites as shown by the Gitlab CI web interface, but also including the integration testing job, whose name is `functional`.

Afterthoughts

System testing for a client/server system has many facets. Here we have discussed several of them, including matching network interactions. At the moment we cannot guarantee that our design has been optimal. Our framework has weaknesses, the most important one is that changes in the environments may cause test failures. For some of the example repositories that we scan, the specified dependency version constraints in the build file can be too weak such that the the replay fails not because of regression, but because dependency version numbers that are detected in new scans do not match the recorded version dependencies. For issues such as these, future improvements can be made, such as having a mock library repository that does not (frequently) update the versions of the libraries it host.

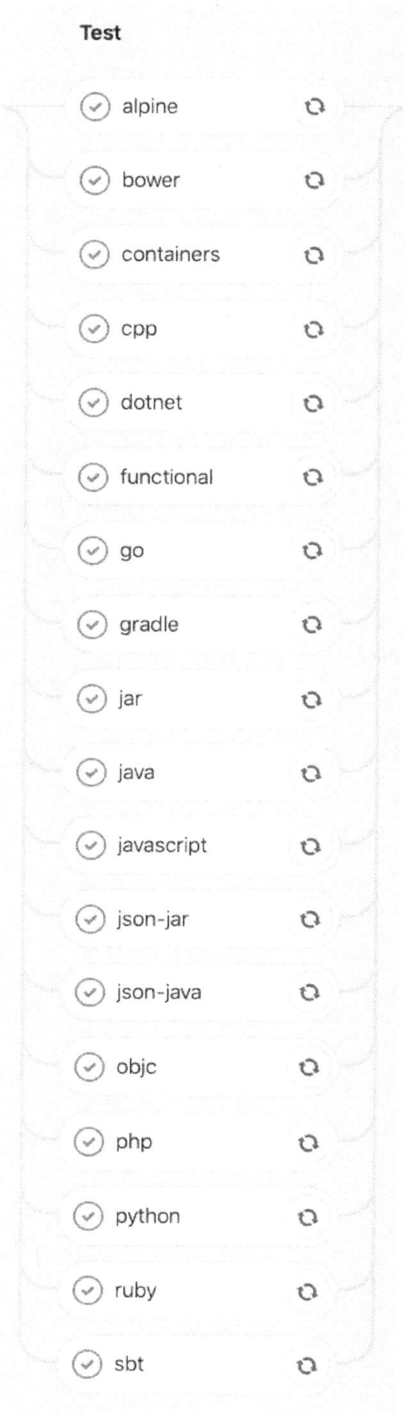

Figure 8: CLI Agent Test Jobs

Contract testing with Pact

Microservices have been gaining popularity in recent years and it is not surprising why. Unlike the traditional monolithic service architecture, Microservices allow you to build an application as a collection of services, each with a specific purpose. For example, you can have an accounts service which manages user accounts and a payments service which manages user payments. As great as Microservices sound, it is not without shortcomings. Among its biggest issues is testing (which is, in fact, a common problem not specific to Microservices).

A common and traditional way of testing services is Integration Testing. In Integration Testing, you start all the services that are supposed to work together and run the databases that they are connected to in a clean slate. There's a lot of setup and teardown involved when running an integration test once. Integration tests are known to be brittle, hard to setup, and take a long time to run. An alternative to Integration Testing is Contract Testing.

What is Contract Testing?

Contract testing is not a new idea but has been gaining recognition in recent years as Microservices become more popular. The idea is to test the agreements (contracts) between API providers and consumers. The contracts define the structure of the API requests and responses which both sides must adhere to. Contract Testing is "consumer driven" (commonly known as Consumer-driven Contract Testing), i.e. the consumer of the APIs will define the requests it will send and the responses it expects and the Provider validates the contracts.

Contract Testing in Veracode

In Veracode, we run many microservices and use Contract Testing to ensure that both the provider and consumer of APIs are communicating correctly with each other. The library we are using for Contract Testing is Pact. We run a self-hosted Pact Broker to help us share the contracts between consumers and providers. We trigger contracts verification with Gitlab webhooks. The diagram below shows the flow from when a commit is pushed to the Consumer project to the complete verification of the contracts by the Provider.

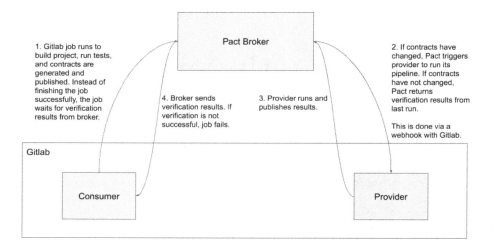

Figure 9: Pact Broker - Gitlab Trigger

The steps that happen can be summarized as: 1. When a commit is pushed to the Consumer service's repository, the repository's Gitlab job compiles, runs the tests, and generates the contract files. Contract files are JSON files generated by Pact. The contracts are published to the Pact Broker and the job waits for the verification results using Pact's command and option `pact-broker can-i-deploy` (see can-i-deploy). 2. If contracts have changed, Pact Broker triggers a new pipeline on the Provider service to run its tests and validate the latest contracts. 3. Provider service publishes the verification results to Pact Broker. 4. Pact Broker sends the results to the Consumer service. If verification was successful, the job passes and the next job in the pipeline continues. If the verification failed, the job fails and the pipeline will be stopped to prevent a release from going out.

Down to the code level

Most of our services are written in Java and to use Pact in our projects, we use `au.com.dius:pact-jvm-consumer-junit_2.12` in our Consumer service projects and `au.com.dius:pact-jvm-provider-junit_2.12` in our Provider service projects.

As an example, consider 2 services that we run - ArtifactService, which provides vulnerabilities-related data i.e. the Provider, and InternalAdmin, which is the backend service for an internal tool i.e. the Consumer.

Consumer defines the contract

Define the rule that uses Pact.

```
@Rule
public PactProviderRuleMk2 artifactServiceProvider = new PactProviderRuleMk2("artifact-service", this);
```

In the unit test, state the Pact to use for verification.

```
@PactVerification(fragment = "artifactByIdPact")
@Test
public void getArtifactById() {
    // tests and assertions for methods that will call the Provider's API.
    // ...
}

@Pact(consumer = "internal-admin")
public RequestResponsePact artifactByIdPact(PactDslWithProvider builder) {
    // Code to convert our data models to PactDsl objects.
    // PactDsl objects are needed for Pact to generate the contracts.
    PactDslJsonBody responseBody = ...

    final PactDslResponse pactDslResponse = builder
        .given("Artifact with id 1 in database")
        .uponReceiving("Request for artifacts by id=1")
        .path("/1")
        .method("GET")
        .willRespondWith()
        .status(200)
        .headers(...)
        .body(responseBody);

    return pactDslResponse.toPact();
}
```

When the tests are being run, for example using `mvn test`, Pact generates the contracts in a JSON file. In our CI/CD environment, this file will be published to the Pact Broker.

Provider verifies the contract

One interesting thing about Contract Testing with Pact is that you do not have to write any test cases in the Provider service to verify contracts. Provider verify contracts by validating states.

What is a state?

As the name suggests, "state" is a condition the Provider is expected to be in when Pact sends a request (generated by Consumer) to test the Provider. This state is essentially the `.given(...)` method as shown in the Consumer's unit test codes above. Think of how during integration tests you need to ensure the database is in a clean slate or whether certain environment variables are set correctly. This is a state.

Run the Provider tests as a Spring Boot Application with PactRunner

```
@ContextConfiguration
@RunWith(PactRunner.class)
@Provider("artifact-service")
@PactBroker(host = "your pact broker url", scheme = "https")
```

```
@SpringBootTest(classes = {ArtifactService.class})
public class ArtifactServiceProviderContractTest {
  // These setup are needed for Pact to know which port the application is running on and thus able
  // to send the requests to.
  static ConfigurableWebApplicationContext application;

  @BeforeClass
  public static void start() {
    application = (ConfigurableWebApplicationContext) SpringApplication.run(ArtifactService.class);
  }

  @TestTarget
  public Target target = new HttpTarget("http", "localhost",
      parseInt(application.getEnvironment().getProperty("server.port")));
}
```

Test the state

```
@State("Artifact with id 1 in database")
public void testGetArtifactById() {
  // codes to insert an artifact with the id into database.
}
```

When Pact runs, it initialises the state accordingly and sends the request as defined by the consumer and compares the response generated by the application with the response expected by the Consumer.

What we like and don't like about Contract Testing

As with all things, Contract Testing has its pros and cons. For us, Contract Testing adds another validation to our tests because we have been using WireMock all the time to run mock servers and generate stub responses in our unit tests. Replacing WireMock with Pact essentially allows us to generate responses in the Consumer project and take it to the Provider for verification. It is also very easy to test the Provider as we just have to initialise the states. However, this also means that the complexity is on the Consumer side as we need to convert our data models to PactDsl objects.

It also integrates naturally with our engineering workflow as we will always need to merge the changes in the Provider service with the verification before the Consumer's build job can pass.

Conclusion

Contract Testing has its merits and so far it has worked well for us. Pact is also a relatively new library but already has support for a lot of languages and its libraries have powerful features such as specifying regexes in String properties in contracts. We think that Pact library will continue to improve and Contract Testing will become more convenient and easier to use. If you are using microservices, Contract Testing (and Pact library) is something you should definitely look into.

Proof Pearl: On the Correctness of Update Advisor

Motivation

We developed a feature at SourceClear called Update Advisor: a static analysis which determines if a library upgrade would cause breakage when applied to a project.

To summarize the approach: given two consecutive versions of a library, $v1$ and $v2$, and a project that depends on $v1$, we first compute a *semantic* diff d between the public APIs of $v1$ and $v2$, then check if the project was calling any of the methods changed or removed in d; if so, we'd label the upgrade *breaking*. The diff is *semantic* in the sense that it takes into account calling relationships.

We wanted users to be able to run this analysis on every commit in CI/CD. However, it involved building call graphs for arbitrarily complex open source libraries, which could take significant amounts of time and memory – we knew this all too well from the experience of building call graphs for our vulnerable methods analysis.

An obvious solution was to precompute these libraries diffs, but what would we store? Real-world libraries can have hundreds of versions, theoretically as many as one per commit. Seeing as a diff could be requested for any pair of versions in the range, storing $O(n^2)$ diffs didn't seem like a good idea.

The solution we came up with was to store a linear number of diffs – only those between consecutive pairs of libraries – and *compose* them on request to derive diffs for arbitrary pairs of versions.

Composing Diffs

What does it mean to compose diffs?

Intuitively, given three versions of a library:

```
// version 1
function a() {
  return 1;
}

// version 2
function a() {
  return 2;
}

function b() {
  return 2;
}

// version 3
function b() {
  return 2;
}
```

- Function **a** was changed across versions 1 and 2, and deleted in version 3.
- Function **b** was added in version 2 and remained unchanged after.

The diffs might look like something this:

```
# diff between version 1 and 2
a: CHANGED
b: ADDED

# diff between version 2 and 3
a: DELETED
b: UNCHANGED
```

Say we're upgrading a user project from versions *1* to *3* directly and need the diff between those. The actual diff is:

```
a: DELETED
b: ADDED
```

It seems reasonable that there must be some relationship between the actual diff and the intermediate diffs we saw:

```
a: DELETED = compose(CHANGED, DELETED)?
b: ADDED = compose(ADDED, UNCHANGED)?
```

A Closer Look

A diff is a set of pairs of an API function and some *diff operation* which describes how the function changed across versions. We define 5 primitive operations: insertion (I), deletion (D), being changed (C), remaining unchanged (U), and being missing altogether (M).

Let's try to figure out the full composition function. There are a few easy ones, but it gets tricky.

```
-- The two from above
compose Changed Deleted = Deleted
compose Inserted Unchanged = Inserted

-- This seems reasonable too: it was a net insertion
compose Inserted Changed = Inserted
```

```
-- Hmm...
compose Inserted Deleted = Missing or Unchanged?
compose Deleted Inserted = Unchanged or Changed?

-- Huh?
compose Inserted Inserted = ?
```

This leads us into what it means for the diff composition function to be *correct*. A working specification could be that each pair of inputs has an unambiguous result, given justification of some kind, and always approximates the actual diff conservatively. The existence of absurd combinations like `Inserted` and `Inserted` is another clue that there is some underlying structure to these operations.

That structure is *whether or not the associated API function of each operation is present in the library versions the diff was computed from.* Say we have library versions $v1$, $v2$, and $v3$. Given an API function f and that the diff between $v1$ and $v2$ has the operation `Inserted`, f must have been absent from $v1$ and present in $v2$. The same argument extends to $v2$ and $v3$. Composing the two insertions then makes no sense because f cannot simultaneously be absent and present in $v2$. It's as if `Inserted` has the type `Absent -> Present`, which prevents it from being composed with itself.

With this intuition, we model diff operations as types (in Idris, because of its magical ability to finish programs for us). An API function is either absent or present:

```
data State = Absent | Present
```

Diff operations have their corresponding types:

```
data Diff : State -> State -> Type where
  Insert : Diff Absent Present
  Change : Diff Present Present
  Delete : Diff Present Absent
  Unchanged : Diff Present Present
  Missing : Diff Absent Absent
```

The composition has a familiar type:

```
compose : Diff a b -> Diff b c -> Diff a c
```

Case-splitting on `compose` and methodically using Idris' proof search reveals that there is an unambiguous answer for most cases; furthermore, invalid cases do not even have to be represented, and Idris allows us to leave them out.

```
compose Inserted Changed = Inserted
compose Inserted Deleted = Missing
compose Inserted Unchanged = Inserted
compose Changed Deleted = Deleted
compose Deleted Missing = Deleted
compose Unchanged Deleted = Deleted
compose Missing Inserted = Inserted
compose Missing Missing = Missing
```

The only cases which aren't unambiguous are those involving `Changed` or `Unchanged`, because they have the same type. As this is a static analysis, we err on the side of caution and pick the more conservative answer – whenever possible, assume something is changed. We could formalize this further with a lattice, but seeing as there as there are only five cases left...

```
compose Changed Changed = Changed -- only thing that makes sense
compose Changed Unchanged = Changed -- more conservative
compose Deleted Inserted = Changed -- more conservative
compose Unchanged Changed = Changed -- more conservative
compose Unchanged Unchanged = Unchanged -- only thing that makes sense
```

This gives us the following table:

	I	C	D	U	M
I	⊥	I	M	I	⊥
C	⊥	C	D	C	⊥
D	C	⊥	⊥	⊥	D
U	⊥	C	D	U	⊥
M	I	⊥	⊥	⊥	M

We are also in a better position now to think about our earlier definitions:

Why not express C in terms of I and D? So we don't lose information. For example, if a function is deleted and later inserted, we want to be able to express that it might have changed.

Why distinguish U and M? U and M operate on functions with different state.

Composition is not symmetric:

```
I . D = M
D . I = C
```

However, it is associative (proven by exhaustion).

Conflating U and M

It turns out that we can conflate U and M into a single operation, *unknown* (?), since they occur in mutually exclusive scenarios. This is useful in practice because when we compute diffs, we want to store just the changes instead of also keeping track of everything that remained unchanged. Also, this doesn't change composition semantics (proven by exhaustion).

Implementing this change gives us the following table.

	I	C	D	?
I	⊥	I	?	I
C	⊥	C	D	C

	I	C	D	?
D	C	⊥	⊥	D
?	I	C	D	?

More details are available in our FSE2018 paper.

Final Thoughts

What does it mean for a function to be correct? Correctness only makes sense in the presence of a specification; here ours was that composition was unambiguous, or that the results were at least justifiable, and would always conservatively approximate the actual diff. I'd say we achieved that here, to the end of gaining more confidence that we could build Update Advisor on the idea of diff composition.

The use of formal methods on day-to-day software problems is still costly enough nowadays that it is not mainstream, and often not as readily applicable as simply writing more (types of) tests, as we have done in the earlier parts of this book. Nevertheless, tools like TLA+, Alloy, or even proof assistants and dependently-typed languages like Coq and Idris are essential additions to one's toolbox; they are useful when the kernel of a problem can be distilled and formalized, so we can be sure the software built atop it has robust foundations.

Dynamic Symbolic Execution with Pathgrind

In this article, we will learn about the technique of *dynamic symbolic execution* and how it can be used for testing and fuzzing binaries. In two previous articles (1,2), we already saw how automated methods can be used for test case generation in Java. Dynamic symbolic execution is an automated approach to generating new test cases based on constraints that are collected from an execution trace. For this article, we will use the Pathgrind tool. Pathgrind is a symbolic execution engine which can be used for automated fuzzing of 32-bit binaries on Linux. Before we jump in, let us first start with some background about symbolic execution.

Symbolic Execution

Wikipedia defines symbolic execution as "the means of analyzing a program to determine what inputs cause each part of the program to execute". The basic idea behind symbolic execution can be explained by the following steps:

- Execute the program with a given input
- Build a symbolic formula during execution which captures the path taken by the input through the program
- Minimally change the formula to create a new formula
- Solve the new formula to generate another input to the program
- Repeat the steps by executing the program with the new input

As an example, let us consider the following `max` method.

```
int max (int x, int y, int z) {
  int m = x;
  if(y>m && y>z)
    m = y;
  else if(z>m)
    m = z;
  return m;
}
```

The method takes as input, three integer values and returns the maximum value among the three. So, calling the method with the input `max(1,3,2)` return 3 as the maximum value. While executing the method we can build the following symbolic formula which captures the path taken by the input through the program. This symbolic formula is also referred to as the path condition (PC).

```
Statement                  Formula
inputs : x0, y0, z0
int m = x;                 true
if(y>m && y>z)             m0 = x0
  m = y;                   m0 = x0 /\ y0 > m0 /\ y0 > z0
else if(z>m)               m0 = x0 /\ y0 > m0 /\ y0 > z0 /\ m1 = y0
  m = z;
return m;                  output: m1
```

In the beginning, the execution starts with the symbolic formula `true` and then continuing for each statement in the program we add a constraint to the formula. Thus, the path condition for the given input (1,3,2) is `m0 = x0 /\ y0 > m0 /\ y0 > z0 /\ m1 = y0`. After eliminating `m0` and substituting the value of `m1` in the formula we get `y0 > x0 /\ y0 > z0 /\ 3 = y0`. This formula captures the path taken by the program for the given input. Now, in order to mutate the formula there are several possibilities: we can negate a particular constraint in the conjunction or we can drop a constraint from the conjunction altogether. For this example let us just negate the first constraint. We get an another formula `y0 <= x0 /\ y0 > z0 /\ 3 = y0`, and we need to check if this formula is satisfiable. This can be done using a number of existing constraint solvers (like STP) or SMT solvers (like z3). The solver tells if the formula is unsatisfiable, or in case the formula is satisfiable it returns the values of the variables in the formula that make the formula valid. For our new path condition `y0 <= x0 /\ y0 > z0 /\ 3 = y0`, the solver gives the following values for variables x0,y0 and z0.

```
x0 = 3
y0 = 2
z0 = 2
```

We can now repeat the same process with these new inputs and carry on the symbolic execution of the program one path at a time. This kind of symbolic path exploration can be visualized with the following execution tree for the `max` method.

Each input that is discovered leads to covering of another subsequent path in the tree. In this case, there are only 3 distinct paths in the program, so just 3 path conditions are required to explore all the paths in the program. For methods without loops or recursion the path exploration is always finite and terminating. However, in general in the presence of loops and recursion a program may potentially have unbounded number of paths. Exploring a program by exhaustively testing all paths in the program can lead to exponential number of test cases. This problem is commonly referred as path explosion, and is one of the limitations of symbolic execution. In order address this limitation, most tools support setting up a fixed depth until which the execution tree is explored and the path exploration process terminates after that depth. A similar strategy is used in pathgrind which we will look at in the next section.

Pathgrind

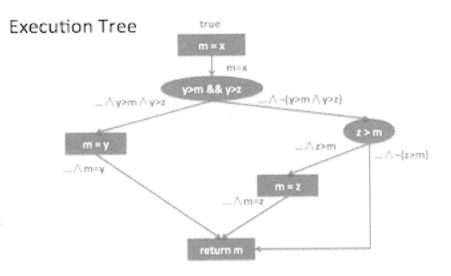

Figure 10: Execution Tree for max method

Pathgrind is a symbolic execution engine based on Valgrind that uses STP for solving constraints. It can be used to fuzz 32-bit binaries on Linux. The installation is fairly simple and detailed in the README.md file on GitHub. Once installed, you need to edit the settings.cfg file to include the following for each program you want to fuzz.

```
[test]
prog       = testcase/test.exe
input      = input.txt
max_bound  = 100
```

The prog parameter specifies the path to the binary and the input parameter gives the file to use for the initial input to start the symbolic execution. It also has an optional max_bound parameter to bound the search during path exploration. By default, pathgrind assumes that the program takes input from a file and generates new files based on symbolic execution to fuzz the program. Once the settings are configured we can just call fuzz.py test to run pathgrind on input configured with test section in the settings.cfg file.

```
user@user-VM:~/git/pathgrind$ ./fuzz/fuzz.py test
[+] expanding execution with file input.txt
    * 4 path constraints (bound: 0)
    * solving constraints [0:0]
    * new_input (1.txt): bood
    * solving constraints [0:1]
    * new_input (2.txt): .aod
    * solving constraints [0:2]
```

```
    * new_input (3.txt): ..dd
    * solving constraints [0:3]
    * new_input (4.txt): ...!
[+] checking each new input
    1.txt[-] argument to program is
    2.txt[-] argument to program is
    3.txt[-] argument to program is
    4.txt[-] argument to program is
[+] scoring each new input
[+] expanding execution with file 4.txt
    * 4 path constraints (bound: 4)
...
Paths Explored: 15
Time Taken: 10.85
```

The output of running pathgrind is shown above. The execution starts with file `input.txt` and new inputs (`1.txt`, `2.txt` etc.) are generated by solving the path conditions (constraints). At the end, it also prints the number of paths explored and the total time taken. While fuzzing, pathgrind generates inputs and executes the binary with those inputs in the hope that one of the input will lead to a memory error and a crash that is detected by valgrind. The crash can be further investigated using the output from valgrind to determine the exploitability of the issue. Thus, new bugs or vulnerabilities in the binary can be found in a fully automated manner.

For the simple test program the fuzzing process terminates in a few seconds, but for more realistic programs of interest like a browser (or the libPNG library) the process can take hours or even days to find some interesting case of failure. This is primarily due to problem of path explosion as mentioned earlier. If we want to see the time taken to execute each path condition we need to install bokeh a Python-based framework for data visualization and just use `plotfuzz.py test`. It will launch the browser and show a running plot of the time taken to solve each formula and the time taken for path exploration (generating new formula).

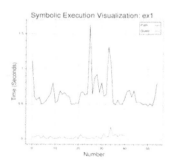

Figure 11: Path Exploration Time Taken

The green line is the time taken in solving the constraint while the blue line shows the time taken in generating new constraints. As is clear from the graph, the time taken to generate new constraints is much larger than the time taken by the external solver (in this case STP) to solve them. I gave a talk on "Visualizing Symbolic Execution with Bokeh" at PyData Singapore earlier this year on this topic. The slides of the presentation contain more examples on how to visualize some of the issues with path explosion in symbolic execution. For instance, if we implement the path exploration of loops in a naive way we will have lots of paths which are similar to each other that represent the unwinding of the loop. The following scatter plot shows what this looks like.

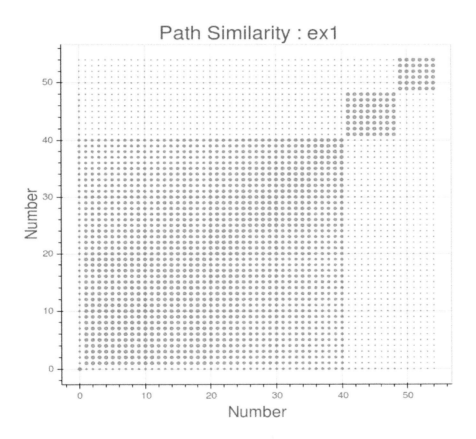

Figure 12: Path Similarity

The size of the dot in the plot depicts the similarity (larger is more similar). All the dots from number 1 to 40 are very similar to each other and represent paths that are not interesting as they come by exploring loop unwinding. Techniques to address such limitations of symbolic execution are beyond the scope of this article and are a topic of active research in this area. With that we have come to the end of this article, more details about how to optimize path exploration with pathgrind can be found in the paper on Exploiting undefined behaviors for efficient symbolic execution. In addition, to learn more about the path conditions, differences between various symbolic execution engines and solvers you can check out the following paper on An Empirical Study of Path Feasibility Queries. If you run into any issues running Pathgrind feel free to submit an issue on the GitHub repo or send in your pull request.

EFDA: a benchmark for software composition analysis tools

At SourceClear, we build tools that help customers detect and manage security vulnerabilities in the open source libraries they use. We constantly ask ourselves this question, "What makes a good OSS management tool?" At the end of the day, we believe, it comes down to data. Up-to-date and reliable data. If your project is using the the latest version of Library A which was published 1 day ago, the tool must be able to detect it. If Library A has 3 CVEs, the tool must be able to inform you of that, at least. If the library has vulnerabilities that are not published to the CVE database yet, can the tool find them?

At SourceClear, we believe data is king. However, even before those data can be retrieved, an OSS management tool must be able to scan the project. Over these years, we have encountered different kinds of project setups that could cause an OSS management tool to fail. The tool might fail to scan the project completely or report a dependency version that is different from what the package manager actually resolves to. Because of this, we created various sample projects to keep track of the languages, package managers, and project setups that our Lightman Scanner supports.

Open-Sourcing EFDA

Today, we are releasing a collection of sample projects as a single open source project called Evaluation Framework for Dependency Analysis (EFDA). The code repo can be found here. This repository will be managed by the Continuous-Security Security project which we will be announcing in a few weeks. In this repository, you will find projects implemented in various languages and with different setups that aim to test the features of an OSS management tool. The projects contain details such as the number of dependencies, whether they are direct or transitive dependencies, and the number of vulnerabilities present. In this repository, you will also find a spreadsheet that lists the features being tested. This spreadsheet allows you to customize the importance of the features and compute a score to determine how well an OSS management tool fits your needs.

Figure 13: EFDA Spreadsheet

Our Guiding Principles

When we set up these example projects, we followed a set of guiding principles.

The basic set of test cases

If we are checking whether a tool supports a particular package manager, what is the minimal set of features we need to test for us to say "yes, this tool supports this package manager reasonably"? Take for example, npm projects. Projects using npm declare their dependencies in package.json. It is common for users of npm to declare version ranges in package.json instead of sticking to a specific version. Another common setup is to separate dependencies into production and development dependencies. How about npm-shrinkwrap.json which helps to lock dependencies' versions? As such, you can find in the npm folder project setups that test each scenario specifically. The same guiding principle is applied when we create example projects for other languages/package managers.

Independent, self-contained test cases

Of course, in a real-world scenario we would expect a project to use more than one feature from its package manager. But we want to make the evaluation process simpler and debugging easier. Each project setup tests one scenario specifically. If a tool fails to report the expected number of dependencies or vulnerabilities for the project, we can safely say that it does not support the feature well enough without digging deeper to find out exactly which feature of the package manager is breaking the tool's analysis process.

Breadth and depth of coverage

There are 2 methods to evaluate a dependency analysis tool. The first method is to look at how many package managers it supports - the breadth of its coverage. The second method is to look at how well it supports each package manager - the depth of its coverage. EFDA checks both the breadth and depth of coverage. This is why at the time of this writing, it has projects implemented in 8 programming languages, 15 package managers, and many more various setups for those package managers.

Configurable weightage of features

Some features may be important to a group of users but not to another group. Some users may not even care if a particular language/package manager is being supported if they are not using them. In the spreadsheet that accompanies the EFDA repository, users can customize the importance (0-5) of each feature. A final score will be computed based on the importance given to each feature.

Contributions

Our goal for releasing this repository is to help everyone who are using open source libraries decide which tool is most suitable for them. You can help make the project better and more comprehensive by adding project setups that are missing in the repository. We look forward to your contributions and comments!

Monitoring as Testing

We've developed our app as sanely as we know how, applied every testing technique in the book, and our app is now live, with data from real users running through it. What comes next?

We're now past the point of detecting bugs early: now we want to ensure that we meet our availability targets, possibly with a bit of bug-finding so we know if things are not working. That's where monitoring comes in: it gives us ways to detect and recover from problems we didn't pick up earlier.

Monitoring is an umbrella term for a number of disparate activities, including the collection and visualization of metrics, management of alerts, or even lightweight smoke tests. They're all valuable and will be needed at some point, but in this chapter we'll focus on the automated aggregation of error conditions.

Sentry features heavily in this chapter, purely because it has an open source product that you can run yourself for free. There are lots of alternatives and everything here applies equally to all of them.

Sentry

As an app runs, errors will occur. We can recover from the expected ones, but because none of us are perfect (and also because our app ultimately runs on real hardware), unrecoverable errors *will* occur. A typical strategy is to log them and move on, because sometimes there really is no recourse but to abort to a known safe point (e.g. terminating the current request):

```
@PostMapping(value = "/jobs")
public ResponseEntity<Void> startBatchJob(@RequestParam(value = "id") long id) {
  try {
    runJob();
    return ResponseEntity.ok().build();
  } catch (Exception e) {
    LOGGER.error("unexpected error", e);
    return ResponseEntity.status(HttpStatus.INTERNAL_SERVER_ERROR).build();
  }
}
```

We might opt *not* catch errors as well, allowing them to go up the stack and be handled by the web framework, or even let them kill the server process and rely on a supervisor process or a cluster manager to restart it. These are more or less the same strategy *because the error disappears into a log somewhere and no one is alerted.*

This is fine for transient errors, but can we guarantee that every error we've ignored this way is of that nature?

Sentry gives us a different strategy. It's a tool for aggregating errors, and it gives us a place to collect data on the kinds of errors that have occurred in the app and analyze it to make decisions.

Prioritization

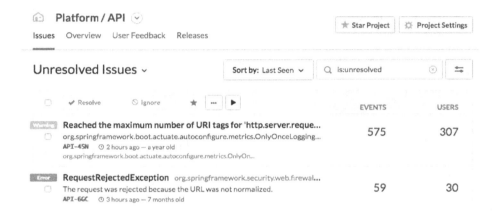

Figure 14: Sentry main page

For a given app in Sentry, we can see a list of errors by type. There are also metrics like the number of affected users and the total number and frequency of occurrences.

Figure 15: frequency

We can use this to tell if an error is still occurring, if it stopped a while ago (maybe someone else fixed it?), or if very long-standing (earliest) or infrequent (graph) issue; maybe then it's not super important that we fix it right now.

Maybe it was a severe bug that affected only a few users, and we want to know who those are – that information is available too.

Sentry also has some bells and whistles around issue tracking, so you can use it for that as well if you don't have somthing else.

Reproducibility

Figure 16: Context

Having context around error conditions is key to reproducing them and coming up with fixes. Sentry captures the exception type, message, and stack trace by default.

User-defined metadata can also be associated with errors, so we can tag them with e.g. the version of the app it came from, or the users affected, or the specific inputs that caused it.

For client-side applications, things like the browser or OS it was running on, the version of e.g. the JVM the app was running on, and even memory dumps can be captured.

Integration

Integrating Sentry into an existing app is straightforward. Errors are sent over HTTP, so they can be sent manually if that's your thing, or in special cases.

A more principled way is to hook into the logging system, which ensures that if errors are handled consistently, they'll all appear in Sentry eventually.

```
<appender name="SENTRY" class="io.sentry.logback.SentryAppender">
  <filter class="ch.qos.logback.classic.filter.ThresholdFilter">
    <level>ERROR</level>
  </filter>
</appender>

<logger name="ROOT">
  <appender-ref ref="SENTRY" />
</logger>
```

Frameworks like Spring Boot provide hooks for handling uncaught exceptions thrown from any controller thread, so they can be logged or handled in a central place. This is perfect for sending them to Sentry. An example integration might look like the following:

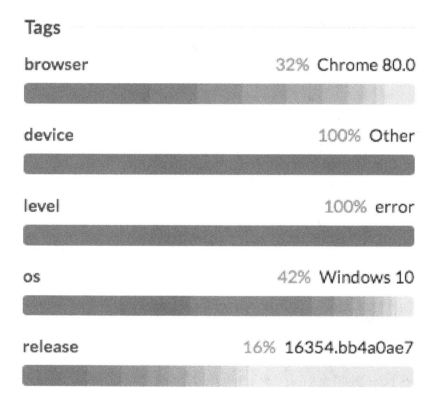

Figure 17: Environment

```
public class SentryHandler implements HandlerExceptionResolver {

  private static final Logger LOGGER =
    LoggerFactory.getLogger(SentryHandler.class);

  private static final Lookup LOOKUP = new Lookup();

  @Override
  public ModelAndView resolveException(HttpServletRequest request,
    HttpServletResponse response, Object handler, Exception ex) {

    // Reentrancy check
    if (SentryEnvironment.isManagingThread()) {
      return;
    }

    SentryEnvironment.startManagingThread();
    try {
      Sentry.getStoredClient().sendEvent(new EventBuilder()
        .withRelease(LOOKUP.get("release"))
        .withSentryInterface(new HttpInterface(request))
        .withSentryInterface(new ExceptionInterface(ex)));
    } catch (Exception e) {
      // No recourse here, unfortunately; is Sentry down?
      LOGGER.error("Sentry failed", e);
    } finally {
      SentryEnvironment.stopManagingThread();
    }

    // Continue with the other configured HandlerExceptionResolvers
    return null;
  }
}
```

Monitoring as Testing

One might see monitoring as a form of integration testing for *unexpected* errors.
This is in contrast to unit tests, which check only for expected errors.

1. Each logging statement of this form

```
try {
  // do something
} catch (E e) {
  LOGGER.error("unexpected", e);
}
```

can be seen as an assertion that the code in the **try** block *does not* throw the
exception **E**.

2. Uncaught exceptions are violations of the implicit assertion that all methods
   in the stack trace *do not* throw.

3. Violations of these assertions don't cause the app itself to crash (as **assert**
   statements would, which is why they can be (and are often) turned off).
   They are, however, surfaced in Sentry.

Continuing the testing metaphor, these assertions have real inputs, unlike the
synthetic inputs one comes up with in unit tests, or the artificial inputs one
gets from fuzzing. This means that if you put in the work to have consistent

error-handling, you can get a lot of mileage out of Sentry and reproducing bugs will become significantly easier.

As an integration testing method, monitoring also finds certain classes of bugs trivially, which is why we recommend using a mix of testing methods and not spending an inordinate amount of time on exhaustively covering paths with unit tests.

Finally, this method of integrating Sentry pairs well with fuzzing, providing a more granular oracle than one would have if relying only on, say, 5xx status codes.

E2E with Cypress

Cypress is an end-to-end JavaScript testing framework for writing and automating UI tests. As of this writing, it runs in Canary, Chrome, Chromium and the Electron browser.

Why Cypress?

Developer Friendliness

Frontend engineers are increasingly becoming more involved in writing integration tests — a shift from previous practices where only QA engineers design and implement test strategies. This means frontend engineers will benefit from testing tools that are specifically designed for their workflow. Cypress fits our frontend engineers' workflow for two reasons: Its debuggability, and its expressiveness.

Debuggability

Being able to run inside the browser means our tests run in the same loop as our application. This translates to better debug-ability. Cypress provides `debug()` and a way of handling `debugger` command and allows us to inspect with browser dev tools. Consider the following simple example:

We want a tab containing the text "Released" to be selected when a variable `releaseStatus` is set to RELEASED. Cypress lets us walk through the different commands and assertions and allows us to "time travel" to see how the interface looks like including how the markups and styles are rendered at certain points in time. Clicking on the FIND command as shown the previous screenshot yields the following in the DevTools console:

This level of control and transparency surfaces significant information for our engineers when evaluating our tests which prove to be handy in implementing or addressing issues. Cypress also provides tools to easily trace where the test fails such as automatic screenshot or video recording.

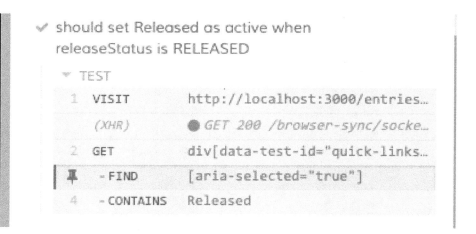

Figure 18: Cypress

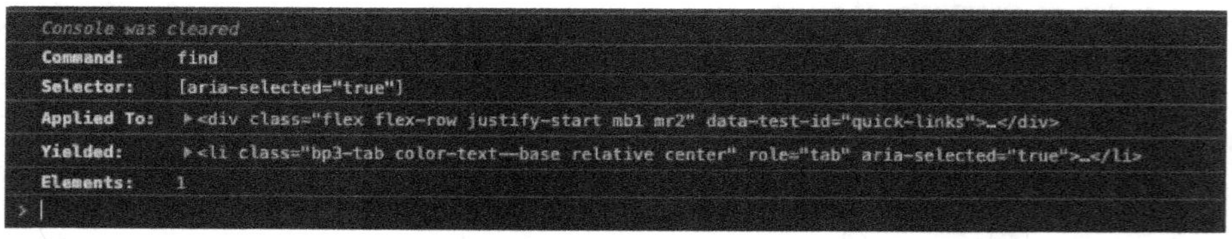

Figure 19: Cypress-in-Console

Expressiveness

Using test frameworks and assertion libraries with APIs that are expressive improves the maintainability of any form of tests. Cypress provides descriptive APIs and its support for Behavior Driven Development BDD and Test Driven Development TDD assertion styles makes writing tests more expressive and intent-revealing.

In the following example, we can easily follow and understand the flow being tested — we visit `http://localhost:3000` , attempt to login with email and password. Then, URL in the address bar should include a `session` parameter.

```
it('logs in',()=>{
    cy.visit('http://localhost:3000');

    cy.get('form')
        .find('[type="email"]')
        .type('my@email.com');

    cy.get('form')
        .find('[type="password"]')
        .type('my-safe-password');

    cy.get('form').submit();
    cy.url().should('include','session');
});
```

In other test frameworks, we might find convoluted sequence of commands or less expressive APIs just so we could achieve the flow above. This is particularly true in cases where additional lines are needed in order to handle waits/sleep with arbitrary numbers.

Less Flakiness

As with any modern web apps, many interactions are implemented to be asynchronous (async). In general, async API calls augment user experience as it provides better feedback about the UI state. However, with async requests, possibility of high latency and slow browser rendering, end-to-end tests tend to yield non-deterministic or flaky results. Flaky tests are tests that pass or fail at different runs. For instance, a test passes under normal conditions but fails when an expected DOM element did not appear in time due to delays in rendering or slow network.

We address flaky tests with Cypress' built-in wait and retry-ability that come by default. Let's take a look at the following:

```
it('should select Libraries tab by default',()=>{
    cy.visit('http://localhost:3000/items');

    cy.get('[data-test-id="tabs-list"]')
        .find('[aria-selected="true"]')
        .contains('Libraries');
});
```

In the example above, we want to test that when a user logs into `/items`, the tab named `Libraries` is selected by default. Here, we need not explicitly call

`wait` right after the `.visit` command just so we can be sure that the DOM is
fully loaded when we perform a `.get` or `.find`. By default, these commands
`wait` and retry to resolve before moving to the next command or assertion.
In this case, `.visit('http://localhost:3000/items');` does not resolve
until all resources (JS, CSS and HTML) have been fully downloaded; And
`get('[data-test-id="tabs-list"]')` will keep retrying until the element
with attribute-value pair `data-test-id="tabs-list"` eventually exists in
the DOM. In Selenium webdriver, similar effect may be achieved with its `wait` and
`until`APIs. For example, `driver.wait(until.elementLocated(By.css('.tabList')));`
. With `FluentWait`, timeout and polling frequency can also produce the
automatic retries. With wait and retry happening by default and wrapped by
simple functions, we do not need to explicitly call them.

Organizing tests

One defining trait that separates Cypress from other end-to-end test frameworks
is its familiarity to frontend engineers being a JavaScript only test framework.
This enables us to easily participate and incorporate end-to-end testing into
our workflow. To further encourage more testing in our team, we organize our
application such that Cypress is installed in the same repo as the web application
being tested as opposed to the alternative of running it from another repo
or service. This lets end-to-end tests to be managed better within the web
application's context where they are written.

Spec Files

We consider each page or view as one test spec and logical grouping of feature test
cases. For instance, login and search pages have their own spec files. There are
cases where tests from different specs rely on shared functions. Some examples are
the auth functions which we want to happen before running tests for login/role-
based views or pages. In such cases, we place those shared functions in Cypress
`support/commands.js`.

Selectors

When writing tests, we augment our JSX markups with the attribute
`data-test-id`. In our code example in the previous section, you find
`data-test-id="tabs-list"` as the selector to get an element. It is ideal not
to use `class` or `id` property when finding elements because these properties
may change as requirements change. For instance, at one point the application uses Block-Element-Modifier CSS naming style where it uses `<div
className="tab">...`, but a new feature that allows new themes to inverse the
style would then need the same element to use `tab--inverse`. Consequently,
tests become brittle as they require change with `class` property changes. Using
`data-test-id` or any reasonable `data-*` ensures that our tests are decoupled

from element properties that may change.

Running in the pipeline

In our CI we set up Cypress to run headlessly. In our Gitlab's `.yaml` file, we first run a stage to perform the initial `npm install` which is then followed by the `npm run test-e2e`. Running `test-e2e` starts the server using `start-server-and-test` library which waits for the server to successfully run first before executing the tests. When deploying to production, we simply instruct our bundler to remove the test attributes `data-test-id` from our JSX markups in our builds.

GramTest: a tool for grammar-based test case generation

In a series of previous articles, we learnt about automated unit test generation using search-based and property-based methods. We also looked at Pathgrind, a tool for dynamic symbolic execution that can be used for automated fuzzing of binaries. Continuing on the same theme, in this article we will look at how grammar-based test case generation works in practice. We also present a new tool - Gramtest. Gramtest allows you to generate test cases based on arbitrary user defined grammars. Potential applications of the tool include automated fuzzing and testing.

Several programs (like parsers, interpreters and compilers) that work on structured input can be tested using grammars. These applications process their input in different stages like tokenizing, building parse tree, converting to AST and evaluating the AST. For such applications, due to the large number of control flow paths in the early processing, random fuzzing does not yield good test cases. Generating tests that exploit the structured nature of the input can provide better results. The simplest way to provide specify the input is in from of context-free grammars.

Context-free grammar

A context-free grammar or CFG is a set of recursive rewriting rules (also called productions) used to generate patterns of strings. As an example, consider the following CFG for arithmetic expressions.

```
<expression>  ::=   <term> <addOps> <expression> | <term>
<term>        ::=   <factor> <multOps> <term> | <factor>
<addOps>      ::=   + | -
<multOps>     ::=   * | /
<factor>      ::=   "(" <expression> ")" | <constant>
<constant>    ::=   0 | 1 | 2 | 3 | 4 | 5 | 6 | 7 | 8 | 9
```

The above grammar captures the language of all strings using four operators ($+,-,*,/$) brackets ($(,)$) and numbers (0-9). The set of symbols that can appear in the strings generated by the grammar are called terminals. We can generate all the strings in the grammar by following the production rules. E.g. for generating the string (1 + 2) * 3, we can apply the following rules:

```
<expression> ::= <term>
    <term> ::= <factor> <multiOps> <term>
        <factor> ::= "(" <expression> ")"
            <expression> ::= <term> <addOps> <expression>
                <term>   ::= <factor>
                    <factor> ::=     <constant>
                        <constant> ::= 1
                <addOps> ::= +
                <expression> ::= <term>
                    <term>   ::= <factor>
                        <factor> ::= <constant>
                            <constant> ::= 2
        <multiOps> ::= *
        <term> ::= <factor>
            <factor> ::= <constant>
                <constant> ::= 3
```

Each string in the grammar starts at the first symbol and then follows the production rules till it reaches a terminal symbol. The rules of the grammar as given above are said to be in Backus-Naur Form (or BNF). It is one of two main notation techniques used for representing context-free grammars. Once we have specified the input to a program in BNF, we can do test case generation by exhaustively applying all the production rules to generate strings. We present Gramtest a tool written in Java that can be used for this purpose.

Gramtest

Gramtest is implemented using the ANTLR4 parser generator. To specify the structure of the inputs used to generate tests we use the BNF grammar available from the ANTLR repository. In addition, there are some useful Maven plugins that we use for our development while working with the grammars. The BNF grammar allows us to recognize any language given in the BNF format. The syntax for BNF can itself be represented with a BNF as follows:

```
<syntax>        ::= <rule> | <rule> <syntax>
<rule>          ::= <opt-whitespace> "<" <rule-name> ">" <opt-whitespace>
                        "::=" <opt-whitespace> <expression> <line-end>
<opt-whitespace> ::= " " <opt-whitespace> | ""
<expression>    ::= <list> | <list> "|" <expression>
<line-end>      ::= <opt-whitespace> <EOL> | <line-end> <line-end>
<list>          ::= <term> | <term> <opt-whitespace> <list>
<term>          ::= <literal> | "<" <rule-name> ">"
<literal>       ::= '"' <text> '"' | "'" <text> "'"
```

The grammar for arithmetic expressions given in previous section fits in this syntax. To generate tests from a given BNF grammar we need to exhaustively enumerate all the strings in the grammar. The Gramtest tool makes it easy to do just that. To run the tool and generate test cases for the arithmetic expressions grammar, we just run the following on the command line:

```
Asankhayas-MacBook-Pro:target asankhaya$ java -jar gramtest-0.1-SNAPSHOT-jar-with-dependencies.jar
-file ../src/test/resources/arithexp.bnf

Generating tests ...
(O*O+O)*(O)*O*O*O+(O)*O*O*O+O*O*O+O*O+O
(O*O+O)*(O)*O*O*O+(O)*O*O*O+O*O*O+O*O+1
(O*O+O)*(O)*O*O*O+(O)*O*O*O+O*O*O+O*O+2
(O*O+O)*(O)*O*O*O+(O)*O*O*O+O*O*O+O*O+3
(O*O+O)*(O)*O*O*O+(O)*O*O*O+O*O*O+O*O+4
(O*O+O)*(O)*O*O*O+(O)*O*O*O+O*O*O+O*O+5
(O*O+O)*(O)*O*O*O+(O)*O*O*O+O*O*O+O*O+6
(O*O+O)*(O)*O*O*O+(O)*O*O*O+O*O*O+O*O+7
(O*O+O)*(O)*O*O*O+(O)*O*O*O+O*O*O+O*O+8
...
```

The "-file" command tells Gramtest to look for the input grammar in the file "arithexp.bnf". By default the generated tests are printed on the screen. In case you want to save them to a folder to use with your program you can use the "-tests" option as follows:

```
Asankhayas-MacBook-Pro:target asankhaya$ java -jar gramtest-0.1-SNAPSHOT-jar-with-dependencies.jar
-file ../src/test/resources/arithexp.bnf -tests generated-tests

Generating tests ...
All tests have been saved in the generated-tests folder!
```

This will save all the test cases in the "generated-tests" folder.

```
Asankhayas-MacBook-Pro:target asankhaya$ ls generated-tests/
1.txt    17.txt  25.txt  33.txt  41.txt  5.txt   58.txt  66.txt  74.txt  82.txt  90.txt  99.txt
10.txt   18.txt  26.txt  34.txt  42.txt  50.txt  59.txt  67.txt  75.txt  83.txt  91.txt
100.txt  19.txt  27.txt  35.txt  43.txt  51.txt  6.txt   68.txt  76.txt  84.txt  92.txt
11.txt   2.txt   28.txt  36.txt  44.txt  52.txt  60.txt  69.txt  77.txt  85.txt  93.txt
...
```

The test cases can then be run with the target program for fuzzing and automated testing. As an another example, lets consider a BNF grammar for generating all strings that have the word "main" in them.

```
<program>   ::=   <letter*> m a i n <letter*>
<letter*>   ::=   { <letter> <letter*> }
<letter>    ::=   A | B | C | D | E | F | G | H | I | J | K | L | M | N |
                  O | P | Q | R | S | T | U | V | W | X | Y | Z |
                  a | b | c | d | e | f | g | h | i | j | k | l | m | n |
                  o | p | q | r | s | t | u | v | w | x | y | z
```

The above BNF grammar uses the curly brackets ("{", "}") construct in BNF to apply the production rule "<letter*>", zero or more times. Running Gramtest with this grammar as input produces strings that contain the world"main" somewhere in them.

```
Asankhayas-MacBook-Pro:target asankhaya$ java -jar gramtest-0.1-SNAPSHOT-jar-with-dependencies.jar
-file ../src/test/resources/main.bnf

Generating tests ...
AAAmainAAA
AAAmainAAB
AAAmainAAC
AAAmainAAD
AAAmainAAE
AAAmainAAF
AAAmainAAG
AAAmainAAH
AAAmainAAI
```

```
AAAmainAAJ
...
```

In addition to the special curly bracket symbols, Gramtest also supports the square brackets ("[", "]") for specifying an optional production rule. While, the parentheses ("(", ")") are used for repeating the rule one or more times. For details on the syntax support please refer to the BNF ANTLR4 grammar that is included with the sources of Gramtest. Hopefully, by now you are convinced that Gramtest is a useful tool to generate test cases from arbitrary user defined grammars.

We will look at some of the details behind the implementation of the tool in a future article. Meanwhile, do let us know your comments on grammar-based testing and please feel free to contribute to the tool by forking it on Github.

Now, we will examine some practical tips to keep in mind while implementing grammar-based test case generation. These guidelines are based on the experience of implementing Gramtest - a Java tool that allows you to generate test cases based on arbitrary user defined grammars. If you are curious about what is grammar-based test case generation, I suggest you look at our previous article on the topic. Let's jump right in on how we implemented Gramtest.

Implementation

The key aspect of the grammar-based test case generation algorithm in Gramtest is to follow all the production rules of the given BNF grammar and then generate strings that conform to the grammar. The production rules themselves form a tree, the root of the tree is the starting rule for generating all the strings in the grammar. For example, consider the following BNF grammar describing all the course codes at a university:

```
<coursecode>    ::= <acadunit> <coursenumber>
<acadunit>      ::= <letter> <letter> <letter>
<coursenumber>  ::= <year> <semesters> <digit> <digit>
<year>          ::= <ugrad> | <grad>
<ugrad>         ::= 0 | 1 | 2 | 3 | 4
<grad>          ::= 5 | 6 | 7 | 9
<semesters>     ::= <onesemester> | <twosemesters>
<onesemester>   ::= <frenchone> | <englishone> | <bilingual>
<frenchone>     ::= 5 | 7
<englishone>    ::= 1 | 3
<bilingual>     ::= 9
<twosemesters>  ::= <frenchtwo> | <englishtwo>
<frenchtwo>     ::= 6 | 8
<englishtwo>    ::= 2 | 4
<digit>         ::= 0 | 1 | 2 | 3 | 4 | 5 | 6 | 7 | 8 | 9
<letter>        ::= A | B | C | D | E | F | G | H | I | J | K | L | M | N |
                    O | P | Q | R | S | T | U | V | W | X | Y | Z
```

In this grammar the rule `<coursecode> ::= <acadunit> <coursenumber>` is at the root. In order to generate the strings in this grammar, we follow all the rules starting from the root (going from top to bottom) to a terminal. When we reach a terminal, we generate a string corresponding to that terminal. For rules that contain alternatives we need to follow all the alternate branches generating strings in an exhaustive manner. Thus, when we run Gramtest on this input it generates the following strings:

```
Asankhayas-MacBook-Pro:target asankhaya$
java -jar gramtest-0.1-SNAPSHOT-jar-with-dependencies.jar
-file ../src/test/resources/coursecodes.bnf
Generating tests ...
ZZX0989
ZZW0989
ZZW0988
ZZV0988
ZZV0987
ZZU0987
ZZU0986
ZZT0986
ZZT0985
ZZS0985
ZZS0984
ZZR0984
ZZR0983
ZZQ0983
ZZQ0982
ZZP0982
ZZP0981
...
```

This simple algorithm based on exhaustive search over the production rules guarantees that we will generate all possible strings in the grammar. However, it may not be feasible to do so all the time. Let us look at some of the challenges with this approach that make it difficult to use it for practical test case generation.

Challenges

In general, a given BNF grammar can contain infinitely many strings due to the recursive nature of the production rules. Recall the following grammar for arithmetic expressions from our previous article:

```
<expression>   ::=   <term> <addOps> <expression> | <term>
<term>         ::=   <factor> <multOps> <term> | <factor>
<addOps>       ::=   + | -
<multOps>      ::=   * | /
<factor>       ::=   "(" <expression> ")" | <constant>
<constant>     ::=   0 | 1 | 2 | 3 | 4 | 5 | 6 | 7 | 8 | 9
```

This grammar captures all possible arithmetic expressions and thus if we blindly follow the rules and generate strings, the test case generation will never finish. It is also possible for a BNF grammar without recursive rules to have an unbounded number of strings if the grammar uses the repetition operator. Due to all these cases we need to find a way to terminate the test-case generation algorithm early, otherwise Gramtest would not be very useful for automated fuzzing and testing.

Practical Tips

We look at three useful ideas that improve on the simple naive exhaustive test case generation and provide a mechanism to address the challenges described in the previous section. All the following three tips are implemented in Gramtest, and if you are curious you can also have a look at the source code.

Tip 1: Restrict the number of tests to be generated

The easiest way to fix the problem is to just restrict the maximum number of test cases that can be generated. In Gramtest, this can be done by using the -num switch. This will ensure that the test case generation algorithm stops after generating the specified number of tests. For example we can generate 10 test cases from the BNF grammar of arithmetic expressions by setting -num 10 as shown below:

```
Asankhayas-MacBook-Pro:target asankhaya$
java -jar gramtest-0.1-SNAPSHOT-jar-with-dependencies.jar
-file ../src/test/resources/arithexp.bnf -num 10
Generating tests ...
(0*0+0)*(0)*0*0*0+(0)*0*0*0+0*0*0+0*0+0
(0*0+0)*(0)*0*0*0+(0)*0*0*0+0*0*0+0*0+1
(0*0+0)*(0)*0*0*0+(0)*0*0*0+0*0*0+0*0+2
(0*0+0)*(0)*0*0*0+(0)*0*0*0+0*0*0+0*0+3
(0*0+0)*(0)*0*0*0+(0)*0*0*0+0*0*0+0*0+4
(0*0+0)*(0)*0*0*0+(0)*0*0*0+0*0*0+0*0+5
(0*0+0)*(0)*0*0*0+(0)*0*0*0+0*0*0+0*0+6
(0*0+0)*(0)*0*0*0+(0)*0*0*0+0*0*0+0*0+7
(0*0+0)*(0)*0*0*0+(0)*0*0*0+0*0*0+0*0+8
(0*0+0)*(0)*0*0*0+(0)*0*0*0+0*0*0+0*0+9
```

Tip 2: Bound the depth of recursive rules

The first tip, though useful, will unfortunately not work for a grammar with recursive rules. While generating the test cases for a recursive rule, we can end up applying the rule again and again (due to recursion) and thus it is possible that the algorithm will not terminate even while generating a single string. To handle such cases we propose bounding the depth of the recursive rule. In Gramtest it can be done by setting the -dep parameter as shown below:

```
Asankhayas-MacBook-Pro:target asankhaya$
java -jar gramtest-0.1-SNAPSHOT-jar-with-dependencies.jar
-file ../src/test/resources/arithexp.bnf -num 10 -dep 1
Generating tests ...
(0)*0*0+0+0*0*0+0*0+0
(0)*0*0+0+0*0+0*0+1
(0)*0*0+0*0+0*0+0+2
(0)*0*0+0*0+0*0+3
(0)*0*0+0*0+0*0+4
(0)*0*0+0*0+0*0+5
(0)*0*0+0*0+0*0+6
(0)*0*0+0*0+0*0+7
(0)*0*0+0*0+0*0+8
(0)*0*0+0*0+0*0+9
```

By setting -dep 1 above, we ensure that when Gramtest sees a recursive rule it will apply the rule only once (follow the rule only once). Typically, we use this parameter in conjunction with restriction on the maximum number of test cases to ensure that the algorithm terminates. The -dep parameter also implicitly controls the length of the generated strings. If we compare the output above with the one under the previous tip where the default value of -dep (2) was used, it is clear that the length of the strings generated in this case are smaller.

Tip 3: Use a minimal sentence generator

If you have a careful look at the strings that are generated above, you will notice that they all exercise only one part of the grammar and they are very similar to each other. For good test case generation we want the generated tests to be more diverse so that they can exercise different paths in the program that is being tested. The quality of the test cases is usually measured using coverage criteria like statement coverage (percentage of statements in the program that are executed by the tests), branch coverage (percentage of conditional branches that are executed by the tests) etc. For grammar-based test case generation, a useful metric is the *production coverage*. Production coverage refers to the percentage of production rules in the grammar that are exercised by the test cases.

For achieving production coverage, we can also use a minimal sentence generator. A minimal sentence generator creates a string with the minimum length that is required for the given production rule. Paul Purdom presented a minimal sentence generator in his classical paper on testing parsers. Although the paper presents the parsers for simple LR(1) grammars, the same ideas can be extended and applied to other grammars. In my paper on Building Extensible Parsers using Camlp4 I describe one such variation of Purdom's algorithm that can be used to test the extensible grammars supported by Camlp4. Gramtest uses a similar variation for generating minimal sentences for BNF grammars.

The minimal sentence generator can be set using the -mingen flag as follows:

```
Asankhayas-MacBook-Pro:target asankhaya$
java -jar gramtest-0.1-SNAPSHOT-jar-with-dependencies.jar
-file ../src/test/resources/arithexp.bnf
-num 10 -dep 2 -mingen true
Generating tests ...
(2*0+9)*(1)+(0)/9
(2*0+9)*(1)+(0)*0
(3+0)-(9)*0
(3+0)-4*1
(3+0)+4*1
(3+0)+4/2
4*(3)+4/2
(3-2)*(2)+(2)*3
(3-1)*(3)-(2)*3
(3+1)/(2)-(1)
```

Looking at the output we see that the generated tests are much more diverse and cover different alternatives in the grammar using smaller sentences.

By using all the three tips we get a tool that is more useful and has practical applications. The default value of the options used in Gramtest are -num 100 -dep 2 -mingen true, but please go ahead and have a look at the source code or play around with the other options. For a given BNF grammar you may get better results with a different set of options. If you have any further tips based on your experience or have any other suggestions on improving Gramtest, do let us know in the comments.

Continuous fuzzing of Java projects with GramTest

Next we will see how you can use GramTest to generate continuous tests that can in-turn be used to fuzz Java libraries and applications.

```
<url> ::=    <httpaddress> | <ftpaddress> | <newsaddress> | <nntpaddress> |
       <prosperoaddress> | <telnetaddress> | <gopheraddress> | <waisaddress> |
       <mailtoaddress>

<httpaddress> ::= h t t p : / / <hostport> [/ <path>] [? <search>]

<ftpaddress> ::=  f t p : / / <login> / <path> [; <ftptype>]

<newsaddress> ::= n e w s : <groupart>

<nntpaddress> ::=   n n t p : <group> / <digits>

<telnetaddress> ::=  t e l n e t : / / <login>

<gopheraddress> ::=  g o p h e r : / / <hostport> [/ <gtype> [<gcommand>]]

<mailtoaddress> ::=  m a i l t o : <xalphas> @ <hostname>

<waisaddress> ::= <waisindex> | <waisdoc>

<waisindex> ::=   w a i s : / / <hostport> / <database> [? <search>]

<waisdoc> ::=   w a i s : / / <hostport> / <database> / <wtype> / <wpath>

<wpath>   ::=    <digits> = <path> ; [<wpath>]
```

As an example we will use the grammar for URLs as defined in rfc1738. Part of the grammar is shown above and as you can see, it if fairly complex. If you directly run GramTest from command line using this grammar as input you will get some interesting test cases:

```
Generating tests ...
mailto:5ol@S*7
prospero://E:4/%Dd
http://c7
nntp:N.p/00
telnet://
news:02
ftp://+n@aF5:21/
wais://B.U/*u/,4_/82=;
gopher://T53
```

This is good for test case generation but not ideal if you want to run a long fuzzing session with some library or application. For doing continuous fuzzing you can use GramTest as a library very easily. The **TestRunner** class provided in GramTest makes it easy to integrate with any application for fuzzing. You can even implement it as part of a test case:

```
/**
 * Test with url grammar
 * @throws java.io.IOException
```

```
*/
@Test
@Ignore("Non terminating test case")
public void testQueueGenerator() throws IOException, InterruptedException {
  final BlockingQueue<String> queue = new SynchronousQueue<>();
  TestRunner continuousRunner = new TestRunner(getClass().getResourceAsStream("/url.bnf"), queue, 10, 8, 32);
  new Thread(continuousRunner).start();
  consumeTests(queue);
}

private void consumeTests(BlockingQueue<String> queue) throws InterruptedException {
  while (true) {
    String testCase = queue.take();
    try {
      URL.parse(testCase);
    } catch (URLParseException e) {
      System.out.println(testCase);
    }
  }
}
```

Just pass the BNF grammar file as input and a `BlockingQueue` to read the generated tests. The queue just makes it easy to add multiple consumers that can each run in their own thread in parallel. This will allow you to run long fuzzing sessions against a target Java library or application. In fact with this exact set up and the given URL input grammar, GramTest found a bug in the Apache Commons URL validator.

If you use GramTest and find new bugs using it, please let us know. Until next time, happy fuzzing!

www.ingramcontent.com/pod-product-compliance
Lightning Source LLC
LaVergne TN
LVHW081803050326
832903LV00027B/2071